Sabu & Me

written by Maura Lane

with illustrations by Hazel Mitchell

Published by Alton Road Publishing a Division of Alton Road LLC

For inquiries, please contact:

www.sabuandme.com

Library of Congress Control Number: 2009903060

ISBN - 10
0615288081

ISBN - 13
978-0-615-28808-6

Printed in the U.S.A.

My name is Maura Lane
and I love my dog Sabu.

This is the story of how our friendship grew
during the first six years of our life together.

Sabu was rescued by my mom as a puppy
before I was born.

When I arrived home from the hospital Sabu sniffed me.

When I started to crawl
Sabu circled around me.

When I began to talk
Sabu looked at me.

When I started to walk
Sabu followed me.

When I played in the park
Sabu ran with me.

When I tossed a stick
Sabu brought it back to me.

When I had dinner
Sabu ate with me.

When I left for school
Sabu hugged me.

When I felt sick
Sabu stayed with me.

When I went to sleep
Sabu cuddled me.

About the authors:

Photo by Julie deLeon

Maura Lane Markowitz
is a 1st grade student at
Lycée Français de Chicago.
Maura's passion is playing with
and taking care of her dog Sabu.

For further information,
see www.sabuandme.com

Her dad is
Jeffrey Markowitz is currently the President and CEO of WheeGO,
www.wheego.com. WheeGO, the find-n-seek game with clues, is as an educational
and exciting game for children. Prior to WheeGo, Jeff was President of a software
technology subsidiary for a Fortune 200 company. Jeff was also an adjunct faculty
member for several business schools in New York City. Jeff lives in Chicago and
Miami with his family Marianne, Maura and Sabu. This is their first book for children

About the illustrator

Hazel Mitchell works from her studio in Maine. She's illustrated many children's
books, plus commercial illustration and painting. Originally from Yorkshire, UK, she
has clients worldwide and her art has been received by the British Royal Family. Mos
days her four dogs and one cat oversee her work schedule.
See more of the artist's work at www.hazelmitchell.com.

About the photographer

Julie deLeon is a garden designer and photographer based in
Chicago. Her design work blends art and ecology in the creation
of urban, roof and landscape spaces. As a photographer, deLeon
focuses on portraiture and landscape photography.
For further information, see www.juliedeleon.com.